The Best of All Possible Worlds

ALSO BY DAMIAN FURNISS

AS AUTHOR:
The Duchess of Kalighat (Tears in the Fence, 1995)
Chocolate Che (Shearsman Books, 2010)

AS EDITOR:
The Captain's Tower (Seren, 2011)
Newspaper Taxis (Seren, 2013)

Damian Furniss

The Best of All Possible Worlds

Shearsman Books

First published in the United Kingdom in 2015 by
Shearsman Books
50 Westons Hill Drive
Emersons Green
BRISTOL
BS16 7DF

Shearsman Books Ltd Registered Office
30–31 St. James Place, Mangotsfield, Bristol BS16 9JB
(this address not for correspondence)

www.shearsman.com

ISBN 978-1-84861-444-4

Copyright © Damian Furniss, 2015.

The right of Damian Furniss to be identified as the author of this work has been asserted by him in accordance with the
Copyrights, Designs and Patents Act of 1988.
All rights reserved.

Acknowledgements
are due to the editors of *The Broadsheet, The Dark Horse, The Journal, The Moth, Shearsman, Stand* and *Stride* where versions of some of these poems first appeared.

Thanks to the trustees of the Mount Pleasant Artists Rest Home where many of these poems were written.

Thanks also to the Mincing Poets for their ongoing critical challenge and support.

*All is for the best
in the best of all possible worlds.*

—Voltaire, after Leibnitz

CONTENTS

1914	The Black Hand Gang	11
1915	Bragging Scars	12
1916	Rasputin's Penis	13
1917	Tom of Finland Station	14
1918	Haemophilia	15
1919	La Grippe	16
1920	The Unreturned	17
1921	The Black and Tans	18
1922	Written by Your Father	19
1923	Stamps of the Weimar	20
1924	Preserving Lenin	21
1925	Horses	22
1926	Fez Is (Not) Fez	23
1927	Rushmore	24
1928	King Zog	25
1929	The Mighty Line	26
1930	Salt of the Earth	27
1931	In the Name of the Father	28
1932	The House of Saud	29
1933	Debutante	30
1934	The Complete Works	31
1935	Gorky's Candy	32
1936	At Lorca's Grave	33
1937	Tomb of the Unknown Author	34
1938	Tea with Mussolini	35
1939	Postcards from Bavaria	36
1940	The Armistice Wagon	38
1941	The Year of Cheerios	39
1942	Tip and Run	40
1943	The White Rose	41
1944	Liberation	42
1945	Blondi	43
1946	Blooming Time	44
1947	Partition	45

1948	Witness Statement	46
1949	Roof of the World	47
1950	The McCarthy Kitchen	48
1951	White Mountain	49
1952	Santa Evita	50
1953	Stalin's Moustache	52
1954	Mau Mau	53
1955	Heart of Belgium	54
1956	Imagine Winston	55
1957	Muttnik	56
1958	Our Man in Moscow	57
1959	Sam and Miss Sam	58
1960	The Kennedy Kitchen	59
1961	Charcuterie	60
1962	Jack and Fidel	61
1963	Bugs Does Dallas	62
1964	A Postcolonial Appropriation of the Hungry Generation	64
1965	The Act of Killing	66
1966	Listen to the Lions	67
1967	Che's Hands	68
1968	Groucho & Co.	70
1969	Cordon Bleu	71
1970	Lulu	72
1971	Postcards from Persepolis	73
1972	Panda Diplomacy	75
1973	La Isla Negra	76
1974	The Undefeated	77
1975	Fang the Sorcerer	78
1976	Bokassa	80
1977	Bunting	81
1978	The Crown Prince of Sealand	82
1979	Tractor Drivers	83
1980	Dog Town	84
1981	Dada in Jeddah	85
1982	The Eye Doctor	86
1983	Threads	87

1984	The Last Man in Europe	88
1985	Wild Nature	89
1986	8½ Feet	90
1987	Rust in Red Square	91
1988	Big Mac and Apple Pie	92
1989	Meeting Dracula	93
1990	The Long Walk	94
1991	House of the Bulgars	95
1992	Speech from the Cage	96
1993	The Hanging Garden	97
1994	Dear Leader	98
1995	The Stolen Child	99
1996	Flea Circus	100
1997	Crabbing with Don Alfredo	101
1998	Brother Number One	103
1999	Tea Party	104
2000	Johnny and Luther	105
2001	The Wind That Drove Men Mad	106
2002	The Last King of Afghanistan	108
2003	Last Post from the Ministry	110
2004	Post Mortem	111
2005	Black Gold	113
2006	The End of History	114
2007	Conversations Overheard in a Soho Restaurant	115
2008	Mr President	116
2009	A Letter from the Romans to St Paul	117
2010	Osama's Pyjamas	119
2011	The Passion	120
2012	The Ten Delicacies	121
2013	Blue Men Sing the Blues	122
2014	A Disagreement Between Ukraine and Russia on the Nature of Poetry	124
2015	The Cartography of Night	125

Notes   126

1914   SARAJEVO, AUSTRIA-HUNGARY

The Black Hand Gang

What if the Gräf & Stift motorcade
of the Archduke Franz Ferdinand
had never taken that wrong turn,
braked, backed up, stalled, etc.
the counterfactual historian
smugly enquires of the lecture theatre.

His students cradle black bombs
the size of grapefruits in their palms.

What if the midget Gavrilo Princip,
stripling son of a Bosnian postman
who lost his right arm to tuberculosis
had not taken aim but eaten his sandwich
or fired that shot and missed the jugular
instead just shaving the royal whiskers?

His students cock their pistols,
sucking pork fat from dumdum bullets.

Let us do some history together. If
that were so, I wager, none of us,
however well armed, would be here.
A weft in the warp of space-time
is torn and the lecturer, his students
and you, dear reader, fizzle into the ether.

1915 LOOS, FRANCE

Bragging Scars

When the duellist detached
the lobe of his ear
it was a clean lunge
made with a clean blade

for a gentleman aims
to the left of the head –
a wedding portrait
is framed from the right –

and knows a man's grace
by the scars he wears,
takes the measure of them,
that each makes his mark –

from the fold of flesh
on a barbed wire fence
with a lungful of gas
in an undone birth

to the thinnest scratch
etched on a face
as poxed and pocked
as this patch of bad earth.

1916 — ST. PETERSBURG, RUSSIA

RASPUTIN'S PENIS

It floats in its jar,
not a pickled cucumber
nor the soaked appendage
of a foaming horse
but the business end
of a monk's gnarly staff,
a shaft that's been places –
cured women of the court
of hysteria, counts and princes
of the more open sort.

They poisoned him enough
to snuff five iron men;
he got up and walked,
they beat him down again;
popped him three times
in the back, neck and head;
had him drowned and burned;
all but this, his last pound of flesh,
a totem preserved in a pickling jar
you see your reflection in.

1917   ST. PETERSBURG, RUSSIA

TOM OF FINLAND STATION

It was hot in that sealed train.
Lenin was coiled like a length of gelignite
in the tight leather shorts of revolt.
Never had he seen so many handsome men
gathered in one place, so late at night.
He handled his bouquet like a bomb.
Seventeen years without pressing his knees
in Russian dirt. Beneath that railway cap
all his hair had gone, but a beard's a beard.
Soft hands pressed rough hands softly,
while the workers stomped their working boots
and danced like there was no tomorrow.
There would be only tomorrow for seventy years,
then the morning after. But that night,
hoisted by sailors onto the bonnet of a car,
Lenin sang 'What is to be done?'
and all the men gathered there sang along.

1918   YEKATERINBURG, RUSSIA

HAEMOPHILIA

In the House of Special Purpose
the Tsar of all the Russias
was forbidden to sport epaulettes,
drink coffee, eat butter
or enjoy his Fabergé eggs.

Reduced to four servants
they retired to the basement
in what was left of Sunday best,
daughters in jewelled corsets,
for a final family portrait.

Alexei was pale as a Siberian winter,
drained by haemophilia,
his sisters wrapping him in the scarves
of their arms, silky and warm.

Anastasia dreamt only of soldiers,
how they flirted with her.
Now their guns pointed in her face
awaiting the order to fire.

'You know not what you do,'
the Tsar said. They knew what they did.
They did it then, with bullets. And then again,
to be sure, with blades, clubs, acid and fire –
all the tools of war.

1919   Massachusetts, U.S.A.

La Grippe

It was war
and it was worse than war:

men with the bones
of other men strung
from the roofs of their lungs;

indigo blue
and mahogany
as the strange fruit
of a lynching party;

and their eyes
and their sweethearts' eyes
ringed rouge red
round blanket grey –

men without guns
wrapped against rain,
stacked, waiting for a train

to breach the peace
with a screech on the rails.

1920 LONDON, ENGLAND

THE UNRETURNED

In the first year of remembering
they were remembered
as the living are remembered

then we raised a cenotaph
out of wood and plaster,
in its hollow – the empty tomb
of an unknown soldier.

When the returning parade
they suggest a greater
march past of the unreturned:

three days to clear Whitehall,
the ghost horses take another day;
it is a week on the Champs-Élysées;
in Germany, they crawl –

a fortnight has passed
and still they worm their way
in this, the second November
after the one before.

1921   Limerick Music Hall, Ireland

The Black and Tans

Tommy took the shilling,
for the shilling he was willing
to bark like a beagle, put on the black and tans.
A dangerous task for Tommy?
Hoist that rag from his jacksie
and parade him down the Falls, walking on his hands.

Tommy likes to travel – check his map,
it's pink as the spud beneath his cap –
that's why the working man of the Tudor clan joins up.
From Templemore to Tralee
he's shat on Calvary
and pissed up the hard stuff in Father Griffin's cup.

Sure as my name is Mickey Nono
they'll be marching with the dodos –
drum the drums, pipe the pipes, wind up the band.
There'll be no more Tommy quips
when his Tommy arse gets whipped,
he'll be spewing from his flue pipe – bloodied, black and tanned.

1922   NORKA, RUSSIA

Written by Your Father

Good beginning
Go you letter from my hand
Go where you are being sent
Go to the best place and show yourself

This summer is so bad
We have to cook with waste
Many did not receive
Nothing did we receive

My dear child
Why you let me to starve
I have asked you many times
Maybe it is not what you think
Perhaps someone has lied

1923   MUNICH, GERMANY

STAMPS OF THE WEIMAR

In my childhood box
stamps of the Weimar
in shades of burnt orange
teach me my first lesson
in hyperinflation.

I am eight years old,
 just coming to terms
with numbers in their billions –

some are overprinted,
their value at dawn
a fraction of their value at dusk.

And on one envelope
the address of a family
whose unborn children
will only ride a train
once in their young lives.

1924   Moscow, U.S.S.R.

Preserving Lenin

Each day we inject under his skin
alcohol infused with glycerine,
flex his joints, the join of his jaw,
and when his face begins to bloom
we dab him with buds of chlorine
to stub out the mould on his chin.
Twice a week, we strip his suit,
dust him down, and wax his hands,
shine his dome like a piece of fruit
and brush powder onto his brow.
Each year, we bathe him for thirty days
in a soup of quinine and formaldehyde –
the broth lacks heart, guts and brain –
then scrub him with potassium acetate,
sponge his cock and balls dry,
reinstate them to 61°, humidity 85%.

1925   LONDON, ENGLAND

HORSES

When Field Marshal Sir Douglas Haig proclaimed the horse had a continuing role in war, that the tank and aeroplane were only accessories to the man and his horse, the veterinary surgeons of the Royal College applauded – their future was secure.

My great grandfather too made his living from the horse, breeding the beasts and training them for war. His methods have been forgotten now: how he tested their blinkered senses with flash and gun powder; burnt pitch and straw to make acrid smoke he would gallop them through, bugle blaring; riding without reins through knee-high mud, to leap hedged ditches for trenches in that stretch of Warwickshire he called Flanders Fields.

At day's end, he took his stiffest brush to their hocks and fetlocks, feeding them crab apples in reward, then slept like a baby in the straw beside them, having fed on peasoup and horsemeat; said it did him no harm, lived to over ninety to tell the tale.

At the end, he said his only regret was never having seen his horses swimming ashore on D-Day, the yeomen of the 9th Cavalry Brigade ready-mounted, silencing the guns of the Hun with their swords, lances pointing towards Berlin.

Fez Is (Not) Fez

So, you say you are going to Fez.
But he who says 'I am going to Fez',
that man is not going to Fez
and he has never been to Fez.
And yet, I know you have been to Fez.
You and I, we met in Fez.
And I know you are going to Fez,
you who say you are going to Fez
and so are not going to Fez.
My friend, when we meet in Fez
I will ask: are you now in Fez
or not in Fez, or in not-Fez,
that un-Fez-like place so unlike Fez
that is nevertheless so like Fez.

1927   SOUTH DAKOTA, U.S.A.

RUSHMORE

Bolsheviks cast in bronze
will rise up one morning,
shed their frosty great coats
and break ice on the Volga;

cities that bear their names
will bear their names no longer;
their names shall be erased
wherever they're engraved.

We've read 'Ozymandias',
we know all things must pass,
statues that were worshipped
are now eye-deep in sand,

but there's a granite mountain
in the Black Hills of Dakota
that stripped of pine and schist
could shape up like our fathers –

hire four hundred hands,
work them for forty years,
give them sticks of dynamite,
spike forty jackhammers,

show the world Americans
can honour their great men,
the heads of four dead Presidents
looking down on them.

1928   TIRANA, ALBANIA

KING ZOG

When the Prime Minister
declared himself President
the President decreed
he be crowned king –
planes rained confetti,
sheep were slaughtered,
two thousand men freed,
two hundred hung.

His palace was superior
to a second string casino
in any minor Belgian resort,
its guest bedrooms
wanting for nothing
but distinguished guests.

The valley men wished
a plague of blind bears
on the men of the valleys –
they needed a strong man
to keep them together,
to hold them apart.

When a would-be assassin
pulled a pistol on him
Zog drew his golden gun,
took aim and fired,
pinning silver medals
with scarlet ribbons
into his assailant's chest,
the ash undisturbed
on his perpetual cigarette.

1929   ALSACE-LORRAINE, FRANCE

THE MIGHTY LINE

'Our playgrounds echo with unborn children.
The mothers of the lost are grey and barren.
Not all men who returned from the last war –
and we here have much to thank them for –
returned from the war they won as men.
My friends, this must never happen again!'
Monsieur Maginot unrolls his master plan,
sketches trenches in the air, baton in hand:
'Here, the last line of attack,' he fences
a ghost, 'must be the first line of defence.'

'Beneath six feet of concrete, Generals,
your mess undisturbed by uninvited shells,
chefs shall enjoy the cool of a kitchen
fully equipped with air-conditioning.'
They raise a toast to the Lion of Verdun
with a Riesling bottled in the Saar Basin,
resolve to reshape the land between Alps
and Ardennes, that the Bosches be corralled
in their tanks, hoiked out like snails,
to amuse the mouth with beurre à l'ail.

1930   GUJARAT, INDIA

SALT OF THE EARTH

'The Mahatma walked
the ghats of Ahmedabad
to the flat pans of Dandi,
took the salt of the sea
in the palm of his hand,
offered it to a country
that was yet to be born.'

Our guide wears khadi
from his cap to his dhoti,
mimes the head blows
of a thicket of lathis
the length of saplings
wielded by striplings
clad in webbed khaki.

'And here is our Gandhi –
last year men came
and thumbed out his eyes,
left him face down
in the watering hole,
licked at by buffalo
and buzzing with flies.'

1931 ANKARA, TURKEY

In the Name of the Father

When they give him his name,
elect him Father of the Nation,
he takes his name as a father
takes a gift from his children:
asks that all his portraits
are hung skewed when he's gone
that the people be reminded
of all he did right doing wrong.

1932 RIYADH, SAUDI ARABIA

THE HOUSE OF SAUD

In the beginning was the House of Saud. And then came the kingdom. And then its king. And the king laid claim to the sand, every grain of it. And the wadis also, for there things grow.

And all the land became theirs. And all that lies beneath the land. And all that is raised upon it. All that flies above the land is now theirs also, and all that crawls below it.

The holy cities are theirs by decree. And the holy places of the holy cities. And all the pilgrims who make their pilgrimage to those holy places. And the taxes on all those pilgrims spend there.

And those who resist, they shall be beheaded in the four cities. And their heads shall be displayed from the high places in every corner of the thirteen provinces. For in the desert, bad seeds do not grow.

And from one king shall spring seven thousand princes. And each of those seven thousand princes, they shall have no more than four wives at once, and do their duty to each, as is decreed.

And the princes shall be given sinecures and stipends. And with those sinecures shall come great palaces. For princes begat princes, each with a mouth to feed and feet to shod.

And those sons of princes shall marry the daughters of priests. And the sons of priests shall marry the daughters of princes. And they shall rule under heaven and over earth.

For theirs is the kingdom, reflecting its glory, for all men. As it has been, and is now, it shall always be. So long as there are stars in the night sky, and the moon sings blue silver to the trees.

1933　　　　　　　　　　　　　　LONDON, ENGLAND

DEBUTANTE

The vagina of Wallis Simpson
was the debutante of its season:

played whiff-whaff for Baltimore
and sang the lead soprano for

the Episcopal Church choir;
her performance of Handel's 'Messiah'

was reviewed as "simply remarkable."
Socialites claimed she was able

to guillotine the tip off
a King Edward cigar, cough,

and smoke it down to the butt,
come up smelling of violets.

But just one 'little man' of the time
crossed her Mason-Dixon line

and was heard to sing
'God Save the King'

as he played north against south
with his weak-jawed mouth.

Taking stock, the Prince of Wales
took a deep breath, then exhaled:

it seemed his darling divorcee
had the best of a he and a she.

1934   Kutama Jesuit Mission, Rhodesia

The Complete Works

Brother, if you were a Jesuit
you'd have known the Boy Mugabe
left crying at the pull-in –
the last bus to Bulawayo
taking his father from him –
would grow up to be President
by the way he herded cows
from the compound to the river
in the first haze of dust –
whip in his whipping hand,
book open in the other –
or his trick of trapping doves
in funnels of strung twigs
hung with jacaranda leaves
and baited with bugs and seeds
to bind their wings with string
as a gift of fraternal love,
and how he read out loud to me
the words we now both know by heart –
poems by Yeats, the Gospel of Mark,
the complete works of Karl Marx.

1935 Moscow, U.S.S.R.

Gorky's Candy

He had destroyed gods
and he had created gods
with the breath of his mouth,
the ink of a pen,

returned from the West
as if the world owed him
all the words in it,
that and the tales they could tell –

a staircase floating
through a light strained through roses
into the library
where books write themselves

and there is Gorky
in a clutch with Stalin
gripping him warmly
by the withered left hand

that steadied the card
he wrote his well wishes in
dispatched with candy
on the eve of *The End*.

1936   GRANADA, SPAIN

AT LORCA'S GRAVE

They've picked at the scabs
healed over, and half healed over,
on the scalp of the hillside
to disinter the relics of his bones

    – no one home –

combed the hill, combed over
all the hills around, for Lorca,
the schoolmaster, and bullfighter –
grave goods and remains – nothing found

    but disturbed ground.

We walk the path he walked
to the crunch of almond husks;
olives are bitter plucked
straight from the branch; my hand

    reaches for your hand

and in the vicinity, a gnarled tree
offers its verdancy of poems,
many by him, or in his name;
my own left near his unknown grave

    then blown away.

1937   TERUEL, SPAIN

TOMB OF THE UNKNOWN AUTHOR

One Sunday in June he set off for Spain.
Told no-one. Had nothing but what he stood up in.
There's no record of his ever having arrived
but for one witness, with him when he died.
They had no weapons, didn't know how
to aim or to fire; had taken the vow
but not yet received the three-pointed star;
could hear where the front was, didn't know how far.
His poems are bombs that never went off.
He killed no-one, was killed by an unlucky shot –
its exit a mouth that offered no prayer.
There's no blue plaque in his hometown square.
His books, never written, remain unread
but are passed around, well-thumbed, by the dead.

1938 ROME, ITALY

TEA WITH MUSSOLINI

Every woman adores a fascist
says Benito's valet, his Roman nose
snuffling out the sweetest
of the honeys licked away,
hoping for a waspish blonde
among the brunette matrons
applying to play Daddy
with the Father of the Nation.

Late afternoon,
a room built for a bigger man:
a blue-stocking poet
is ushered in between
one tailored suit and another,
goes down in supplication
to a man who keeps his mutz
and spur-heeled boots on.

Then tea and cake
in the mirrored hallway
with the Roman-nosed valet
while back at his desk, Il Duce
turns the pages of power
licking his still honeyed fingers,
the picture above him
soon to be hung upside down.

1939   MUNICH, GERMANY

Postcards from Bavaria

Odeonsplatz, 2nd August 1914.

In the world before world war
on that last day of peace
a postcard seller's hawked
the last of his scenes,
is drawn to the square
by the word on the street.

He hears the lion roar
and it's hats in the air,
a spring in his feet,
an icon of wrong
    illuminated
as if the sniper upstairs
had cracked a shot of light
when dark would have done,
pasted a face in the crowd –
    by some miracle
imagine the camera was a gun.

1939   MUNICH, GERMANY

The Bürgerbräukeller, 8th November 1939

When the Beer Hall exploded
war ended before it began.
Imagine the scene: Hitler
slicing the air, the spit
of his mouth spraying the crowd
and then the ceiling caving in,
body parts flying around.

Georg built the infernal machine
in the false bottom of his carpentry box;
hitched the movements of two alarm clocks
to the winker of a Volkswagen Beetle;
packed powder, a battery, detonators
into a hollow in the swastika-draped pillar
that framed the manic Führer
as he exhorted the Old Guard to war
for thirteen minutes too short.

1940   COMPIÈGNE, FRANCE

THE ARMISTICE WAGON

He is here, and so is history:
hands on hips, he twitches furies
with the wishbone of his limbs,
then pumps his fists in reckoning:
There is a map scratched on his eyes,
an irritant of border lines:
Alsace-Lorraine is German now,
the coastal ports from Calais down
to Brest and all their hinterlands –
he shunts his armies on the plan
south and west, grants Italy
the east; then occupies the wagon-lit
to cast out last war's ghosts. Dictation done,
he makes his mark, and is gone –
commands his men raze the clearing,
haul Foch's carriage towards Berlin.

1941   Golden Valley, U.S.A.

The Year of Cheerios

The head of Bugs Bunny first popped out of the rabbit hole to ask Elmer Thud 'What's up Doc?' in January 1941 when the British captured Tobruk from the Italians; Benghazi and Tripoli followed before the Afrika Korps arrived to begin their tug-of-war with the Desert Rats; Montgomery and Rommel both loved Bugs.

Cheerios, the first oat-based, ready-to-eat breakfast cereal, were launched onto the American market in May 1941 when the Deputy Führer flew solo to Scotland in an attempt to negotiate peace with Great Britain on the eve of Hitler's declaration of war on the Soviet Union; Rudolf Hess ate Cheerios each morning in Spandau.

Dumbo, Walt Disney's animation featuring a baby elephant ridiculed for his big ears who learned to fly by using them as wings, was released in October 1941 when the German army continued its push towards Moscow forcing all the Soviet government but Stalin to flee to Samara; Stalin slept with a picture of Dumbo next to his bed.

1942   Exeter, England

Tip and Run

Some said the rats had left town
two hours before the sirens howled
on a magic carpet of fur and fang
as if they'd had an early warning;

that the people took to the hills
singing hymns to keep the chill
from their bones, drown the echoes,
blackout that incendiary glow;

and the horses worked hard that year
hauling timbers out of the fires
even as they burned; wrapped in tarps
our tribe made wigwams under the stars.

1943   MUNICH, GERMANY

THE WHITE ROSE

Now I find my good men
are gathered in the night
to wait in silence,
muffled in a fog
of empty phrases.

In the time of harvest
the reaper cuts
with wide strokes –
note their names,
none will go free.

1944   PARIS, FRANCE

LIBERATION

We visit Paris in mid-winter
though its fall was in late Spring:
in the second rush to the sea
barely a shot was fired in the city
but when the Wehrmacht marched
the length of the Champs-Élysées
the sky was battleship grey,
would stay so for four long years.

The sunlight was a liberation
when the Free French crept
into the city that August dawn
with not an African among them;
no negro American put his boot
into a collaborator's crotch;
and if there were Jews, the sites
of internment went unremarked on.

History is swept beneath our feet
but men alive then live today
and what do they remember now:
good time girls kissing their GIs,
full on, then, a few days later,
those guilty of horizontal collaboration
being bundled down St Michel,
heads cropped shorter than fashion allows.

1945 BERLIN, GERMANY

BLONDI

They debated the method for days:
a shot to the head would spoil her face,
but muffle her mouth with a pillow
and feathers would fly in the spat:
chose to award capsules of cyanide,
tooth-sized, to each man of rank,
each dog of distinction; cracked
one between her canines, watched
her gums bleed blue. She was mourned
more than the children were mourned.
They lugged the newly weds, dead,
wrapped in bunker issue blankets,
laid them out on their honeymoon bed,
a foxhole dug by Russian shells,
Blondi spread across her master's legs,
the family burned to molar and bone.

1946   TOKYO, JAPAN

Blooming Time

Across the four seas
all are brothers.
In such a world why
do the waves rage,
the winds roar?

Hirohito recites
his grandfather's poem
over and over,
staring down the trumpet
of a phonograph recorder:

as Emperor he'd ordered
the bombs not to fall,
two bombs had fallen –
the bark is black this year,
a deficit of leaves,

skin flakes of ash
drifting beneath
the cherry trees
soft as pink blossom
at blooming time.

1947 SHIMLA, INDIA

Partition

He had a good dinner
with Nehru and Jinnah
while the Mahatma fasted and span;
drew lines, called them borders,
but lines don't give orders
and a map's not the same as a plan.

1948   NEW DELHI, INDIA

WITNESS STATEMENT

It was 5:12 in the evening
when I met the Mahatma Gandhi.
The air had the promise of Spring.
I greeted him with a namaste.

When I met the Mahatma Gandhi
he was leaning on his nieces.
I greeted him with a namaste.
This is my statement as a witness.

He was leaning on his nieces.
He wore his homespun dhoti.
This is my statement as a witness –
my name is Nathuram Godse.

He wore his homespun dhoti,
I was stood three feet away.
My name is Nathuram Godse,
I didn't hear what he had to say.

I was stood three feet away
when the gun fired three times.
I didn't hear what he had to say.
I was at the scene of the crime.

When the gun fired three times
it was 5:12 in the evening.
I was at the scene of the crime.
The air had the promise of Spring.

1949   Siachen Glacier, Kashmir

Roof of the World

Riding the Leh highway
from Kashmir to Ladakh
we surf the roof of the world
hugging the line of control
fifty years on the edge of war.

We are on the edge of history
with lightning dancing on the peaks
and thunder that might be monsoon's end
or the beginning of a fifth and final war
rumbling the bass bin of the Siachen.

The day peace broke out
I wonder if they touched gloves up there
or stamped that peacock dance,
scratching a line in the snowpack
with a swagger stick's brass end.

1950   WASHINGTON, D.C., U.S.A.

THE MCCARTHY KITCHEN

In the heart of your home
enjoy perfect control
and night-time privacy.

Here, the good housewife
ploughs the only iron
with a built-in headlamp,

dreaming of a utensil
that can whip, mince and grind –
turn leftovers into soup.

Whatever your budget
choosing your cooker
is like choosing a partner –

in the prickled display
of the cocktail stick
and pickled gherkin

she is only attracted
by the whitest of whites
owing to the advent

of fluorescent lighting.
She loves the singing
of her friendly kettle.

White Mountain

Although we live in Europe's house,
in a wet room, by the sea,
no poet has yet had the nous
to versify its bureaucracy

and if one did, let's call him me,
what would he tell us all about
our brothers in one currency
but quietly what others shout:

that those who live together need
agree some rules to keep the peace
but a postcard's worth should be enough
not this white mountain of the stuff.

1952   BUENOS AIRES, ARGENTINA

Santa Evita

Dr Ara the master embalmer
took the corpse of little Evita –
long a martyr to cancer –
emptied her skull, made of her
the world's most beautiful cadaver.

Dead Eva went to the cinema
as the date of a military officer
to watch a Latin Count Dracula
fandango with doppelgängers
as limp and bloodless as her.

On the balcony of Casa Rosada
she'd danced a solo lambada
in a cast of bandage and plaster.
They say the light leaked from her
as from a weeping Madonna.

In the barrio of La Boca
a rosary bathed in her tears
cured the mothers of hysteria
as if those true believers
had touched the wounds of a healer.

Then the generals banished her
to the hills of Monza e Brianza –
put under in the name of another
she longed for her long lost lover,
got not so much as a visitor.

At last they disinterred her
as you might uproot a flower,
delivered her to the gardener
who pruned and preened, soon made her
more like a rose than ever.

Back home they entombed her
beneath a ton of alabaster:
pressed thin as a wafer
of the body of Our Saviour
a weight was lifted from her –

and her hair was blonder
and her skin was paler
and her heart was lighter
than all who went before her
and all who'll follow after.

1953   MOSCOW, U.S.S.R.

STALIN'S MOUSTACHE

Those nights at the dacha,
with the spirit inside him –
his waxed moustache
could've saved the world.

Feasting through the chill hours,
Moscow is as he imagined it,
one of the Tsar's treasured jewels
winking in a basket of bread.

At dawn he dismissed those
less worthy than himself, then me.
A guard is always on watch.
I spent my nights watching him.

I watched as he stumbled into bed.
I watched as the slackness got inside his head.
I watched him piss himself where he fell.
His watch said six-thirty, I stood by until twelve.

1954   THE WHITE HIGHLANDS, KENYA

MAU MAU

A neighbour steals your ox,
takes his panga
and carves a toothless mouth
across its throat,
hangs it out to bleed,
lays a fire to roast its meat,
falls to feasting with his friends.

The next year,
famine has passed,
a new calf is fattened,
all is forgotten.

A stranger steals your land –
the land that cradled your father,
the land that buried your mother.
Each path is a line on your hand,
each stream a blue vein.
Where there was sky, he raises a fence,
puts guards on the gate.

The next year –
watchtowers and wire.
Remember that panga?
It knows where you are.

1955   BRUSSELS, BELGIUM

HEART OF BELGIUM

Lumumba had been to Belgium,
he had seen white men
taking their comfort from the sun.
At night they drank and sang,
whether it meant war or peace
Lumumba could not tell –
he was taking his message to the world.

He desired to have kings
meet him at railway stations;
he intended to accomplish
    great things;
when he smiled a door opened
his people wanted to walk through –
freedom, freedom for the Congo.

It took days for the report
to find its way home:
a middle-aged negro
found in a muddy hole
with a hole in his head.
The voice had gone. Nevertheless
he had given them a piece of his mind.

1956   CHARTWELL, ENGLAND

IMAGINE WINSTON

Imagine, if you will, the phone rings
and it is Winston Churchill, bored
and keen to raise hell. Sir Winston
is not to be trusted: he is a violent man
prone to wearing overalls at breakfast;
his underpants smell of stale cigars.

No matter, he is a chap you greatly admire –
beat the Germans, always wears apt hats –
so naturally you agree. He has a devil
of a job firing up the pilot light, so decides
instead to take cup cakes with dry martinis
in a gazebo on the croquet lawn, play Bezique.

A canary sings from Winston's mohican.
Gout fills out his handmade boots.
He talks fondly of the great and good
dictators. He misses his valet. He wishes
he could turn back the centuries, enjoy
all those bloody wars he missed out on.

1957   Baikonur Cosmodrome, U.S.S.R.

Muttnik

There were dogs in space
and the dogs remember them:
Gypsy, the stray, retired and settled down;
Snowflake was launched six times yet survived;
Seagull and Little Fox were atomised.

Laika, meaning 'barker', barked her last
in a hot tin can, circling the earth,
but then dogs will do what any fool commands:
she wagged her tail from kennel to craft,
fed up on Epsom salts and high protein gel,
massaged with iodine and alcohol.

My little bug, you weighed 11lbs,
barely more than a baby, when you shot across the sky,
orbited, stone dead, two thousand times,
span to earth with your tail in flames,
never to hit the ground.

1958   Moscow, U.S.S.R.

OUR MAN IN MOSCOW

Van Cliburn had rehearsed
through the owl hours of the night,
the span of his blurred hands
pounding Tchaikovsky's octaves
and the tone poems of Rachmaninoff
as Sputnik bleeped overhead.

A heart the size of Texas,
he played for an hour in one breath,
the froth of his rockabilly quiff
spilling over the black and white keys
while women pressed the lip of the stage
offering him their roses.

Three decades on, his fingers sang
'Moscow Nights', Gorbachev and Reagan
singing along; his shirt of purest white
snow melting over the boards;
a lone bear stranded by the thaw
in the Piney Woods of Fort Worth.

1959   WALLOPS ISLAND, U.S.A.

SAM AND MISS SAM

Sam wipes his brow with a salute,
embraces Miss Sam, herself due in space,
tenderly, and then, if astronauts can speak,
which they can, speaks of how it feels to float
twenty leagues up, and then out at sea,
sewn into his suit, strapped into a cone,
while the world's greatest navy combs
the waves to bring him back to ground;
of how they should mate face-to-face
now a monkey has penetrated space.

1960   WASHINGTON, D.C., U.S.A.

The Kennedy Kitchen

A reason to rejoice
came with the abolition
of the flimsy fashion apron.

The one-room career girl
eats her fork meal
from a tray on her knees,

her grandmother astonished
by her sucking up dust
from the wipe-clean lino.

Gay. Bold. Distinctive.
Hers is the era
of mocha and cream.

Day after day
she makes with her hands
the gift of love:

just pick-up and squeeze her,
she's soft as kid leather
and warm to the touch –

in the breakfast nook
below the work surface
you've never had it so good.

1961 PARIS, FRANCE

Charcuterie

They rise from the mud
like rats in a flood
the Seine throws up:

Algerian corpses
spicy as sausage
or other charcuterie –

the coiled white pudding
hung by gendarmes
from the Île de la Cité

where we watched the butchers
watching the butchery
on the Pont Saint-Louis

doing their business
in wipe-down aprons
with wipe-down batons

and the outsides of men
and the insides of men
fell from the sky.

1962   Havana, Cuba

Jack and Fidel

When they dropped brown acid in the air conditioning
his broadcast went on without a blink:
he railed against kamikaze molluscs,
the bacilli dusting his wet suit,
exploding golf balls and booby-trapped baseball bats:
said they should settle war on the field of sport,
square up and fight like men.

Back on the domestic front
Jack had paid due regard to the potency of cigars
but Fidel possessed an unimpeachable nose,
could sniff out the fatale in any femme;
handed her the gun from beneath his pillow,
asking whether it was love or war
she was looking for, which side of the bed
she liked her eggs buttered on.

By the time he was done, her legs were trembling.
You Yankees, once you've had Latin
you never do WASP again, he said,
handing her a bullet, its copper jacket
etched with the Kennedy name,
stroking the beard only time would grey
and tug from his handsome chin.

Bugs Does Dallas

Texas is as vast as Texas –
all those geysers spewing oil,
skyscrapers scraping the sky,
and cows hungry as Continentals
chewing up the great plains.

Another day on the campaign trail
when even blue seems grey
but for the clowns on the grassy knoll
juggling Korea and Vietnam, North and South,
while Mafia dons fall about laughing.

Motorcade One jack-knifes the corner,
a bearded babushka filming the show
with her Super 8 cine camera.
The three stooges are present and incorrect,
drinking early in a boxcar on Railyard West,

while Biffo the Cuban Buffoon
in red mohair wig and grease paint
pulls black dogs from his stove pipe hat
and Buttons the Badgeman, sporting
the pin of every clown convention

since cousin Coco took Lincoln down,
pings off a head shot from his trampoline
tumbling in time with Bam Bam
the Umbrella Man, who nonchalantly
pumps his brolly up and down. High noon.

Who'd have guessed, tucked in Bugs' tickling stick
with a string of ruby hankies was a magic bullet?
Not Mr President, dreaming on dead blondes.
Governor Connolly, maybe, but only when
lung sucked shirt through a hole in his chest.

Or Jackie – pill-boxed in baby pink –
crawling the trunk of the limousine
to reach out for Jack's skull cap and brain
the day the circus came to town.
And the world stopped. And then started again.

1964   KOLKATA, INDIA

A Postcolonial Appropriation of the Hungry Generation

Mother,
I was born
not wanting to be born,
descended
from a wrong womb with a wrong name.

Father,
I am secretly
keeping watch on my activities.
Let me tell you
I am readying myself to die.

Mother,
snip in rage
with hot metal pincers,
lick the sunbeams
from my fingernails.

Father,
keep this eyelash
wrapped in pink paper,
I will split into pieces
for the sake of art.

Mother,
I confess
I've forgotten women during copulation
in a procession
of wet and slippery organs.

Father,
I want to see
my own death before I pass away.
Roll the rug,
push me off a running train.

1965　　　　　　　　　　　　　　Medan, Indonesia

The Act of Killing

It was not the fact that he had killed
that needled my eye. My neighbour upstairs
has killed twice, with shots to the head.
Nor that at first, though guilty, he expressed
not a tremor of regret. My neighbour upstairs
goes about his life, and sometimes laughs.
Neither that he killed with his soft hands,
braver somehow than at distance with a gun.
Eye contact. The pulse. That final breath.
No. It was that he really wanted to re-enact
the killings he had done, and then commit
his script of a thousand cuts to cine-film.
Wear makeup. Change costume for each scene.
Sometimes a man, sometimes a woman's part.
The murderer and victim, he played both roles.
Then the retching. And then the credits roll.

1966 KINGSTON, JAMAICA

LISTEN TO THE LIONS

When the Conquering Lion of Judah
touched down in Jamaica
he was greeted by the furthest flung
of his far-flung tribe, raised his hand
to reveal, if you were there, a stigmata,
and so the prophecy was fulfilled:
Christ will return as a king,
reign over the promised land
and all shall fall prostrate before him,
the lion lying down with the lamb.

Back home in the Jubilee Palace
the lions of the Lion of Judah
dine daily on the meat of zebra,
their big cat eyes as soulful
as any predator unable to prey.
Listen to the lions, how they purr
as they paddle their paws on his chest
armoured with medals and braid,
and slurp at his imperial face
as a sheep laps at its young.

1967   LA HIGUERA, BOLIVIA

CHE'S HANDS

Che's grave is not Che's grave.
And the bones in it are not Che's.
And those cold hands in the jar
tucked away in Fidel's pantry,
they are not the hands of Che,
though they are both human
and Che-like. And that wax mask
that impressed the face of Che
did not impress the face of Che.
And those photos of the dead Che
as Christ, with the generals playing
Romans, display neither Christ,
nor Che, nor Romans. And his wounds
are not wounds as we know them.
And if you are the man who killed
Che when Che said 'Now you must kill
a man,' then you are not the man
who killed Che, for you are not a man.
And all the tales of Che you've read
are not tales with Che in them.
And all these Che poems are not
Che poems, or even poems at all.

Che's name is not Che's name.
He was neither born nor did he die
Che. The name of Che was not chosen
by Che, but chosen for Che, although
Che chose it for himself, signing
himself Che. And if you took a lock
of the hair of Che, it is Che's hair
no longer. And if you wear a Che
t-shirt, then you do not wear

a t-shirt Che would have worn.
And if you sport a Che beret,
more fool you. And if you say that Che
was a saint, you either did not meet
that Che or you have never met
a saint. And any likeness at all between
my Che and your Che is coincidental,
if you believe in coincidence, which
Che did not. And if you say Che
lives, then Che lives, although he
doesn't live, and isn't Che. And if
I say Che never lived, then that
is all I have to say about Che.

GROUCHO & CO.

They are old now
and browning in the sun
on the four-week beach
oystering the Seine,
their walrus moustaches
frothed with the beer
of a Left Bank reunion.

When the Vespers bells
of Notre Dame clang
they lug their bellies
across the Pont des Arts,
cursing the love locks
bracketing the railings,
the keys tossed away.

Back in the Latin Quarter
they fill a favourite bistro
that served their stomachs well
in the bloody days of May
even as cobbles were prised
from the Roman streets,
the beach beneath still burning.

Yes, life has been good to them.
You can read in their complexions
the nights of wine and roses,
short days and long vacations.
And if they want anything, it is this –
the right to raise a fist, kiss
the men they've now become.

1969   SAIGON, VIETNAM

CORDON BLEU

Wearing the whites of Escoffier
Ho Chi Minh learned the techniques
that make up *haute cuisine* today:

how the brigade system depends
on each chef flashing his blade
in good time, to the same end.

At night, he rode the dumb waiter
from the dim of the Carlton kitchen
to the land of crystal chandeliers,

pop-up tactics the Viet Cong –
tunnelling deep behind enemy lines
with Hanoi knives – took on,

taking their profession seriously
as the *pâtissier* Ho Chi had been,
his fingers crimping the *pâté bris*

the way Escoffier had done
to serve the yankees with green tea
on the day they flee Saigon.

1970   ADDIS ABABA, ETHIOPIA

Lulu

If owners look like their dogs
or dogs look like their owners
the lapdog of Haile Selassie –
Root of David, through the line of Sheba,
Grand Master of the Elders of Zion,
giver of the rod of correction,
Grand Cordon of the Order of Solomon,
Knight of the Bath and the Garter –
had the head of a shaved terrier
and the body of a starving Chihuahua.

But when Lulu's pampered paw
petted the foot of a footman
that footman was seen no more.
And he who the lapdog pissed on,
the piss wiper wiped his shoes
and shined to the Emperor's satisfaction;
the feet of that dog and its master
never needing to touch the ground;
the bearer of fifty two cushions
having a comfort for every occasion.

1971   TEHRAN, IRAN

POSTCARDS FROM PERSEPOLIS

14th October 1971

'Five times five hundred years
shahs warmed this peacock throne...'

the steward lectured us busboys
and waiters, each of us with a degree

in the sciences of French cuisine,
the arts of English hospitality.

They planted a forest in the dust
to shade the royal guests, infidels

we served truffled quail eggs,
and mousses of buttered crayfish tails,

an oporto ring of figs and cream,
and tulip of cognac Prince Eugene

with sorbets of Dom Perignon champagne
lightly dressed with the spittle of shame.

1st February 1979

When he returned
we returned:

tar on the streets
bubbled with blood

and the oil of roses
where petals were ground

by ten million feet
on the trail of his robe.

The road was made flesh,
his car a mound,

as the chopper raised
him out of the crowd

and a hostage of words
fell from his mouth.

4th June 1989

I'd give a hand to the wrist
for a hair of his beard

or this arm to the pit
for a chip of his tooth

for each tatter of shroud
a patch of my skin

but when he's hauled,
unswaddling, over the crowd

blades of the chopper
whipping our blood

he's pale as a newborn
dropped in the dark

somewhere between
heaven and earth.

1972　　　　　　　　　　WASHINGTON ZOO, U.S.A.

PANDA DIPLOMACY

Chairman Mao resembled a panda –
roly-poly from extras at dinner,
eyes ringed from the ministrations
of his ever eager young nurses –
while the cuties chewed on bamboo
he rubbed his teeth with green tea.

'Do as the Empress Wu did,'
he instructed, 'Send Satan pandas.'

Darling Girl and Shining Star
were greeted like pop stars
when they waddled from their crates,
then they attempted to mate
Tsing-Tsing slipping his penis
into Ling-Ling's purse-like ear.

'What do we give in return?'
Nixon asked Kissinger.

They settled on Milton the musk ox
as an exemplary American male.
He worked hard to provide for his wife,
Matilda, to build her a good home,
before dying of hardware disease
having swallowed too many nails.

1973 EL QUISCO, CHILE

LA ISLA NEGRA

He got the words down,
Neruda, the right words
in the right order,
saying the right things,
drunk on the sea.

And when they came
he knew full well
what they would burn
and what they could not
and would never burn

and that was enough
to die for, that, and the love
of a good woman,
and an apple, fat and juicy
as a just bitten moon.

The Undefeated

The war has ended, the leaflet said. But it had fallen from the sky, and from the sky came the enemy. Letters from friends, pictures of his family, a notice of surrender from the fourteenth army, all forgeries.

The Americans disguised themselves as fishermen and farmers, lived as if war had been won. He decapitated one, made him watch himself die as a warning to the others.

Relief came in the shape of Norio Suzuki, a young man in search of a big story. Hiroo taught Norio how to trap a bird, wring its neck, roast it stuffed with roots and herbs. In return, Norio showed Hiroo the latest camera, how it took pictures of the two of them on a timer. For the first time in quite a while, Hiroo smiled.

But it was only when his commanding officer arrived to stand him down that Hiroo's war was over. 'Whatever happens, I'll come back for you,' the Major had said. It took him almost thirty years.

Hiroo sheathed his sword, handed it over; his type 99 rifle, still in good working order; the dagger his mother had given him, engraved with the words 'never surrender'.

Fang the Sorcerer

On Christmas Day the President gifted himself a double dose of iboga. His bark shredder shredded his bark. His shred grinder ground his shred. His grind stirrer stirred his grind. His cup taster tasted his cup. He nodded, eyes bulging. All was good.

As the national anthem faded, the President addressed the nation. In this way, the order was given. Across town his henchmen – all dressed in santa hats – went about their business with abandon, rounding up his enemies, inventing new ways to kill them.

The priests who failed to proclaim his image the only miracle were crucified sideways.

The minister for statistics had his body cut into little pieces to teach him how to compute.

The former lovers of his current mistresses were forced to eat their own genitals.

Officers of the military were buried standing to attention and had their faces eaten away by ants.

The jailbirds of Blackbirch danced his praise songs until they collapsed from exhaustion.

Those wearing spectacles were trucked to the national stadium and hung, Mary Hopkin warbling 'Those Were the Days' at them.

The last of the intellectuals gone, the word was removed from the dictionary. The dictionary was removed from the library. The library was removed from the city. When he left, the lights were turned out, being deemed no longer necessary.

They found him in the forest eating bugs and worms, deaf and blind to the world, wrestling with his demons. He had the national treasury in a suitcase under his bed. The trial was short, Macias Nguema sentenced to death 101 times, for a sorcerer has 100 lives.

1976   KINSHASA, CENTRAL AFRICAN EMPIRE

BOKASSA

The man Jean-Bedel Bokassa,
Head of the House of Bokassa
in the line of Dobogon Bokassa,
parades down Avenue Bokassa
to the Stade des Sports Bokassa
self-crowned Emperor Bokassa
by the then President Bokassa
and is applauded by all Bokassas –
the thirty-one uncles of Bokassa,
the nineteen wives of Bokassa,
the fifty-five children of Bokassa –
bringing shame on the name Bokassa
and all those who bear that name.

1977   LONDON, ENGLAND

BUNTING

When the Queen's septum was pierced by a safety pin, my childhood ended, youth began early. Come Jubilee, rival symbologies went truncheon to fist in a Bank Holiday rumble, the last day the Union Jack was flown in anger.

The Sex Pistols' single 'God Save the Queen' reached Number One that weekend, Auntie attempting to rewrite history by installing Rod Stewart in the top spot, as if his leopard skin g- string was a better example to the young.

Come Holiday Tuesday, I was snatching plastic soldiers from the sky as they drifted down on parachutes the size and shape of Steve Jones' knotted handkerchief. One of them, we were promised, had a ten pound note attached, and I was determined to get it.

Meanwhile, on the Thames, Johnny Rotten screeched at the Palace of Westminster, his chartered tug, *The Queen Elizabeth*, surrounded by police launches, coppers with loudhailers low in the mix, their searchlights illuminating his leer.

Twenty-five years on, Robbie Williams sang 'Let Me Entertain You' at Buckingham Palace, accompanied by the drums and trumpets of the Coldstream Guards, as succinct a Situationist statement as an old punk could imagine.

The Crown Prince of Sealand

He took on the force
of the oceans, talked
its waves down to size
and when they disobeyed,
violence the only recourse,
of course he used violence –
a slap, the threat of a gun.

If a storm blew in
the royals bunkered down
in an underwater tower –
listened to the whir
of propellers, the call
of a humpback whale –
plotting the next scheme

to fill their coffers:
issue stamps at top dollar,
coins in gold and silver,
flog peerages and follies;
all the burdensome business
of governing a kingdom
at war with wind and tide.

1979   TIRANA, ALBANIA

TRACTOR DRIVERS

In his 79th volume of memoirs
Hoxha remembered Stalin,
the minutes of each meeting so dull
they are an antidote to insomnia
still prescribed in Albania
by doctors who know better than drugs.

His appeals to the youth of the Soviets
to return to the one true path
were bitter as a priest muttering to himself
three Our Fathers and one Hail Mary
after the last pope has pronounced
the unerring death of God.

Back in the day, they sat thigh to thigh
watching 'Tractor Drivers', a musical comedy
set in Manchuria, the warmth of red wine
like a shared tartan blanket on a Balmoral picnic,
the Queen and Prince Philip both fans,
like Hoxha, of the slapstick of Norman Pitkin.

1980   LIMA, PERU

Dog Town

Once there were people here.
Then, no people – only dogs.

Guerrillas moved in. Painted symbols
and slogans. Moved out, red-handed.

Soldiers moved in. Whitewashed
the walls. Withdrew, pale-faced.

When the army killed a guerrilla
they fed him to the dogs.

When the guerrillas killed a soldier
they fed him to the dogs.

The dogs didn't take sides.
They ate what they were given.

'Murder is meat' they barked,
growing fat and content.

There were dogs here,
then there were no dogs.

They hung from lampposts
blinking, like unexploded bombs.

1981   Jeddah, Saudi Arabia

Dada in Jeddah

Retirement has been good to him:
days spent in praise
of air conditioning, Mercedes sedans,
push-button phones; nights on his knees
tending the surviving wives;

popping out once or twice a week
for shipments of cassava, groundnuts and beans;
300lbs of Ugandan meal and bone
pushing his trolley down the Panda aisle,
testing the tenderness of halal meat;

then back to the shag pile, chintz and chrome
minding the barbecue on his patio,
rustling an extended family feast
to the jig of a bagpipe drone.

1982   DAMASCUS, SYRIA

THE EYE DOCTOR

Looking into the eye
he saw a perfect design –
would take a blade
to the sight of a bull,
peel away the iris
and peer through its pupil
to probe at the weakness
of its blindspot.

'This is how we govern,'
his father tells him
gripping his own eyeball
in a pincer of thumb and finger
to calibrate pressure,
'Observe carefully, know
your capacity for pain,'
he says, dripping humours.

1983 SHEFFIELD, ENGLAND

THREADS

I loved a Sheffield girl, six when the bomb dropped; although she and the city survived, whenever I relive *Threads* I mourn her passing as if it happened, and she was dead before I knew her, one of those bodies abandoned at the Fir Vale Infirmary.

I was seventeen on the day of broadcast, wore an armour of CND badges; even at six they wouldn't have impressed her, nor protected me from the devastation. But each marked a moment of reflection on the horrors to come.

The flash of a nuclear blast leaves its shadows; each unfortunate witness has its image burnt on their retina. When I first met her, that face put the heat on me for days, milk bottles melting on the doorsteps as I loped home through the dawn.

That film began to play in my head again when I first saw her wearing rubber gloves, soft flakes of snow painting winter scenes outside the kitchen window; I let her clean up after a meal I'd cooked, just so I could watch her from behind.

She was too young to know the world had ended, humming as she scrubbed, the sky dark before its time, my hoping the drift would keep her from going home. When she curled up to sleep alone, she could have been a sofa model.

The next night came, our time to celebrate being alive. In the year the Cold War was over, she was thirteen, old enough to consider our collective mortality, just as she no longer had to. We were yet to meet, but I was relieved for her, and waiting.

THE LAST MAN IN EUROPE

Song trickles from the telescreen:
The Chestnut Tree is empty now,
the lonely hour has struck fifteen –
let's go to where the bluebells grow.
Today is April's coldest day –
the thrush will sing to please itself –
tomorrow is the first of May,
meet me beneath the chestnut tree.

Meet me beneath the chestnut tree,
tomorrow is the first of May –
the thrush will sing to please itself.
Today is April's coldest day,
let's go to where the bluebells grow.
The lonely hour has struck fifteen:
The Chestnut Tree is empty now,
song trickles from the telescreen.

1985   MONTANA, U.S.A.

WILD NATURE

Inside your head
King Ludd is sleeping
in his backwoods cabin
in Lincoln, Montana.

He lives on nothing
but his wits, tracks prey
and digs bitter herbs
from the dying land.

Listen, he is stirring
from dreams of equations,
the hives on his belly
a call to action.

You hear his muttering
rising in volume
as he wires his latest
device for the mail

and it has your name
penned on its packaging
and you are awake
when the postman rings
     and rings again.

1986   MANILA, THE PHILIPPINES

8½ Feet

She built a palace for her shoes
and when she was gone
they built a museum for those shoes
she left behind:
four pairs for each day of the year,
matching gowns and handbags
each scented with Mad Moments
by Madeleine Mono.

A quarter century on,
first the storm, then the flood:
espadrilles drilled by termites
float among the kitten heels
and sharkskin sling backs
embossed with the crossed Cs of Chanel,
sandals in soft napped suede
abandoned in tornado mud.

1987   Moscow, U.S.S.R.

Rust in Red Square

When the German Mathias Rust –
an eighteen-year-old amateur
with fifty hours fly time –
landed his high-wing Cessna
among the unmarked Ladas
in full view of the Kremlin
the Marshal Minister of Defence
and Commander-in-Chief of Airspace
had no choice but throw himself
on the longsword of Stalingrad

for there Mathias was on video
in a bright orange jumpsuit
and cheap aviator sunglasses
laughing with shoppers and tourists;
and if you were young then, as I was young,
you knew anything was possible –
to lose your virginity,
your mind to politics and philosophy,
receive the keys to your first plane or car,
and prompt the end of an empire.

1988 — BELGRADE, YUGOSLAVIA

BIG MAC AND APPLE PIE

When the golden arches
were raised over Belgrade
Slavs queued round the block
to eat like Americans.

More grist in the meat
and chaff in the dough
than the QA man was used to,
the recipe for ketchup

took some translating,
and the perfection of Little Gem
was not easy to replicate
in the slug fields of the Sava

but if they wolfed their food
too fast they vacated the tables slowly,
liked to smoke contraband,
sit and while away the day

pulling circus faces
at the squirt-guns in the government
necessitating the employment
of clowns whose only function –

to hustle sag-arsed loiterers
out of their bucket seats
back to the tail of the queue
at the fag-end of the street.

1989   BUCHAREST, ROMANIA

MEETING DRACULA

That long autumn
in the Spring Palace
drained and languid
on a velvet day bed
I feared for my tongue
if the vampire gags ran dry.

Elena spooned me
carpaccio of something rare,
stroking my neck
and petting my ear,
while Nicolae rehearsed,
polishing his hair.

But when he turned
from the gilded balcony
his jowls were ashen –
they'd laughed at his fangs,
jeered at his cape,
mocked his chilling stare.

1990   CAPE TOWN, SOUTH AFRICA

THE LONG WALK

Through the window of our haveli
India is reflected in Pichola Lake
its beauty not distracting us from TV,
the camera trained on a prison gate
and Mandela's long walk to freedom
coming towards us like the lava
of a twenty-seven year eruption.

I walk across the water
and into the souks of Udaipur
to be deloused. A portrait of Gandhi
hangs in a marigold draped line
with the barber's immaculate father,
while my head in the mirror, the third in a triptych,
is clipped to a buzz cut – all the rage
on Robben Island, both sides of the cage.

1991   MOUNT BUDLUDZHA, BULGARIA

HOUSE OF THE BULGARS

We live the best of possible lives
at the best of possible times
in the best of possible worlds –

our way of truth in light
writ large in the polished concrete
and tin plate effigies
of the House of Bulgarian Communists

scalloped like a spacecraft
landed on Mount Buzludzha
from an ancient future
to take the statues home –

men of bronze and stone
stumbling from their squares
with barely a wave goodbye.

Once they were few
and then all were one by decree,
Georgi led blinking onto the balcony
to announce revolution to the nation.

Now grates where there were flames,
the graffito across the gateway –
    'forget your past' –
itself fading into history.

In time to come, families gather here
to picnic in the snow –
look longingly at the sky.

1992   LIMA, PERU

SPEECH FROM THE CAGE

The day before the hotel exploded
I was sipping a Pisco Sour;
the day after, reading a newspaper;
on the front page, the scene
I'd snapped my own face in
had been clumsily rearranged.
In between, guerrillas had descended
bearing gifts from the Andes,
put the town I was now in to flame
and blown all the bridges away.

On the Island of El Frontón,
the man we knew as Presidente Gonzalo
scratches in his cage, his revolution
jacked-up on syringes of insulin
and submarines stuffed with cocaine.
Judges in hoods bait him with writs
while he waves his pudgy fists
to make his speech from the cage,
bleating like a tethered goat, the kind
a mad dog would make a good meal of.

1993   BAGHDAD, IRAQ

THE HANGING GARDEN

In his water garden
he had songbirds
hung in cages:
their beaks wired,
heads hooded,
legs looped with iron.

His first son
took the pulse of a quail
with his fist,
let it fall to earth
and lie there, jerking,
to chill in the sun.

His second son
fed a pair of doves
to his pair of lion cubs,
their little roars
nothing more
than baby yawns.

While at table,
their father ate
his cold cuts
whistling birdsong
with his fingers
and his teeth.

1994   PYONGYANG, NORTH KOREA

DEAR LEADER

When Kim read the prophecy
three swallows fell from the sky –

the third son of a third son foretold
a triplet child would fill

his rack of khaki safari suits,
empty his cellars of champagne,

step into his stacked size threes,
and ride the armoured train.

Rewarding such fertility
with plated knives and golden rings

he took them into custody;
housed in spartan dormitories

underground, lukewarm and grey,
they rocked to praise song lullabies;

visiting in the dead of night
he read them bedtime stories.

1995 DHARAMSALA, INDIA

THE STOLEN CHILD

He had been seen in dreams
and in his dreams
he had seen the dreamers
'clear as the day
the sky fell to earth,'
his mother said, expecting them –
the call of conch and drum.

'When teacher becomes student
there is joy in return.
All I know, I owe to you
as the sun shines on the moon,'
a monk read from the scroll
the words of the Dalai Lama
to the reincarnation of his master
while the child touched his ear.

That stolen child, carried away
to not even the gods know where,
and on his empty chair
wrapped in an unworn robe
the last known photograph
of the boy he's left behind –
fading before our very eyes.

FLEA CIRCUS

San Cristóbal de las Casas is a town in Chiapas that was named by a poet. The focal point of the Zapatista rebellion, when peace broke out it hosted the pow-wow. Then came lessons in asymmetric diplomacy: the government cavalcade was hemmed in by a scattering of drawing pins.

Outside the palace of palaver, an iron ring of knitting women sold popped corn in cones of old newspaper, smudged with the headlines of the New Year's Day two years before, when rebels had taken the town and all those around it, an occupation that lasted for almost twenty-four hours.

We joined the great waiting, settling down to watch a flea circus, scratching our way through the performance as ticks were put through their paces, jumping through hoops a hundred times their height, hauling little wheeled carts a thousand times their body weight.

When Marcos arrived on his motorbike, the strays of the town began to mate. With a two piston salute, he dismounted, the smoke rings emanating from his pipe signalling the heir to the moustache of Zapata and sombrero of Pancho Villa was ready to parlay.

Ten years later, the subcomandante was still talking, telling the tale of his crippled rooster – Penguin – who travelled Mexico with him, looking for a white-bibbed waddler to toddle off into the sunset with, an egg between her legs, the sky painted a permanent red.

I'm not sure what he was saying, but liked his way of saying it; maybe that's why they tolerated him, those indios, a honky professor in their midst, surrounded by long-haired gringos, talking bird shit.

1997   BRASILIA, BRAZIL

CRABBING WITH DON ALFREDO

Thursday night is crab night
chez Don Alfredo,
he picks his victims
by the boxing of their claws,

loves how blue steams red,
his liver spotted hand
first on my knee
and then on my thigh.

Unrolling a wrap of velvet
he admires himself
in the surgical steel
of his pliers, mallet and blade;

twists to break off the crustacean's legs
and prises apart the shell
to get inside its cavity,
spreads its innards on the plate

and separates flakes of flesh
to lay one on the fur of my tongue.
We lick fingers, smack lips
and toast Ascunción

as he whisks away his napkin
to reveal a striped linen blazer
free of ribbons, brass and braid.
'Tomorrow we eat oysters, fresh,'

he croons as we part,
left framed by the door,
erect, the presidential wave,
a halo of mosquito wings.

1998   Anlong Veng, Cambodia

Brother Number One

He said: 'Be mindful of breath'
and then breath left
the burning of his chest

in a white plume of smoke.
I lit a cigarette,
slugged the whisky he kept close.

The pyre was his own hair
stuffed mattress,
eight tyres, a wicker chair

we decked with pink sprays
of fuchsia, lit the fire,
stood by, then dwindled away

to one. I saw his clenched fist
rise from the flames
as the shells fell about, missed.

These were his words at the end:
'Time is our friend,'
he said. Time is not our friend.

He had no watch, forbade
us wearing watches;
he watched us – we obeyed.

We'll hand his wife his bones.
He had the smallest
hands of any man I've known.

1999   SURREY, ENGLAND

TEA PARTY

Each year, at this time of year,
since they had retired, or were retired,
Augusto and Margaret take tea:

his place, always; she punctual
as his pacemaker's silent clock;
orchids, a box of Harrods chocs;

a kiss on each powdery cheek,
her eyes a rheumier shade of blue
than in his failing memory.

She performs the ceremony:
pours oolong tea served black
in a china delicate as a bone.

They discuss the films of Jean-Claude
Van Damme, the campaigns of Napoleon,
their least favourite grandchildren,

the roses they've had named after them,
who will attend whose funeral parade,
how smoke is safer than the spade.

2000   Karen Hills, Burma

Johnny and Luther

The Lord first spoke to Johnny and Luther at the age of nine, granting them their first magical power – to kill by thought alone. A policeman died that day, the teeth in his face smashed in to a tombstone grin.

At ten, the band of brothers had grown to five-hundred, supplemented by four-hundred-thousand invisible comrades, immune to bullet and mine. Travelling on the backs of their minders, the boys directed operations, smoking cheroots as offerings to God.

By eleven, the twins could recite the Bible from Genesis to Revelation, though they had never read it, nor learned to read. It taught them many things about the Chosen People, by miracle invincible and invulnerable – they had nothing to fear but their mother's tongue.

At twelve, doubt set in: they no longer feared God, although He still feared them. In the silence of their bamboo clearing, the fronds of fern a gauze to the aching sun, wrapped in a bandage of mist, there was only silence now, but for the hissing of oil, six feet below ground.

2001   NEW YORK, U.S.A.

THE WIND THAT DROVE MEN MAD

It slipped into New York
ice-packed in a crate
with the pollock and the mullet
the halibut and hake
and the mutant fish that don't yet have a name –
they said Chernobyl was to blame.
The port, it stank way worse than bad
when they popped the cork that had
plugged the wind that drove men mad.

At first, the climate went unchanged.
Just a gust, then a low flying plane
burst onto the scene, stealing the show.
That's the way this wind blows.

It curdled up the Hudson
as it cut a line inland
turning tables over tables
playing brass in marching bands
and twirling majorettes around like batons –
now that's intelligence to act on –
the gridiron crowd, they cried *Zindabad!*
when it swept into the Ronald Reagan stand –
all hail the wind that men drove mad.

The danger behind a do-not-enter sign
has just been bowled over by a Force 9 –
that breeze is just a prophet before the coming messiah...
Man, this wind's on fire!

It swung right through Manhattan
like its towers were made of matches

lit up and smoked a stogie;
brothers run, but not one catches
the last D-train – it's been cancelled.
Air Force One's being scrambled.
'Pops, it was cooked up by bad men in Baghdad',
says Agent W to his dad.
'Christ, we'll nail that wind if it drives us mad.'

But it's immune to every form of defence –
do your worst, it'll make no difference –
it swallows satellites, spits out all the cables –
this wind is Cain vs Abel.

Now it's knocking at your door
like a long-lost friend.
You peep through the peep hole, unsure –
perhaps the world is on the mend –
and then, there's no door there at all.
The ceiling's blown away. And so have all the walls.
Call the Bank of Mum and Dad.
I've got bad news. They too have been had
by the wind that drove men mad.

And you're staring it in the face.
Your eyes sting like they've been dipped in mace.
You'd call a friend, but have forgotten all their names.
The wind has changed the game.

Then this fear gets inside your head.
It's the fear of fear itself, the doctor said.
Wake up! Who's that next to you in bed?
Ring them bells! Bring out your dead!
The wind is collecting door-to-door,
leaves a notch on your bedpost, keeping score.
Now even Peter upstairs is sad
to report the Pearly Gates have had
a run-in with the wind that drove men mad.

2002 KABUL, AFGHANISTAN

THE LAST KING OF AFGHANISTAN

He was eight feet tall
and wore a set of whiskers
that skirted the skirting board

bathed in Neapolitan mud
with the women he liberated
to ease his lumbago

and played Buzkashi
only on Tuesdays
to save the pashmina

preferring wild golf,
his extensible clubs
the wonder of the nation.

The leaner on Allah
of the god given kingdom
in the rule of the uncles

was a mountain lion,
the people worshipped
each hair on his toes –

brush the ceiling
from the floor of his palace,
bring the roofers in

for when the President calls
he will crawl the ocean
to be among us again

in his lambskin cap
his Italian suit
and his iron underthings

for who will be left
when the empires are gone
and we are all alone?

2003   BAGHDAD, IRAQ

Last Post from the Ministry

They are bombing us with pencils:
sharpened, they fall from the sky.
These pencils are booby traps –
ignite in the hands of small children
to scribble their faces with carbon –
but they are not pencils, these pencils,
they are not in control of anything,
they are lost in a desert of paper,
make no use of a compass,
cannot even write their own names.
These pencils are lying every day,
they are lying always, and mainly
they are lying. We will defeat them
with facts and figures. Where are they,
these lying pencils – they are nowhere.
They could have been removed.
They could have been hidden.
They could have been destroyed.

2004   RAMALLAH, PALESTINE

POST MORTEM

When he scrubbed his teeth –
crooked and broken –
with a brush bristled
from the spine of a camel
did he twig the white paste
was laced with polonium?

And as for the soap
on his baby pink flannel
did a midnight valet
lather the leather
with ambergris spewed
from a nuclear whale?

Or did servants infuse
his dandruff shampoo
with thallium blue
to fleece his fine comb
and clog up the flue
of his wistful half-smile?

We'll take a scalpel
to this body of questions,
subject tissue samples
to our calibrations,
dispatch the findings
to doctors of medicine

for theirs is the oath –
Hippocratic, ethical –
that undoes time,
is divine intervention,

irradiates crime
and denies hypotheticals.

2005   ASHGABAT, TURKMENISTAN

BLACK GOLD

Be good as gold, my little ones,
and watch my gold-cast statue turn
to the golden light of early dawn
and on through the gold of day until
I'm molten in the setting sun.
This is my golden day, my golden month –
gold star! – you named time after me.
I ask you, why do dogs chew gold?
To gild their teeth and strengthen gums!
So yank the gold out of your mouth
and melt those nuggets in my pan.
Throw your gold rings and bracelets in,
where you have piercings, give them up.
Have your gold wrought in my flame –
I shine eternal under moon or sun,
the source of light you lend my name.

2006   Washington, D.C., U.S.A.

The End of History

'This is the end of history,'
the lecturer blithely announces
to his fellow historians
gathered to mark its passing.

The historians exchange
nervous glances – without history
there is no study of history;
without study, no lectures;
without lectures, no pay cheques,
students, student pudenda etc.

One gestures this is nothing
but a grand gesture. Another
fails to convey his statement
is empty of meaning. A third
wonders just whose class
voice this mouth is voicing.
While a fourth proclaims
the man on the lectern
to be a great man, that his theory
is set to change history.

Then the historians go to war
and the history war goes on
until historians are no more –
there is blood on the stain proof carpet,
guts down the wipe-clean walls –
though history goes on as before.

2007   LONDON, ENGLAND

CONVERSATIONS OVERHEARD IN A SOHO RESTAURANT

I dread to think what it's like after dark –
Damien's already drunk at the bar –
and this place was once the house of Karl Marx?

Tony's sat out back with his bodyguards
while Gordon's boys dine at the Gay Hussar –
I dread to think what they're like after dark.

David runs faster than his Jaguar!
That 'geek' is Michael, he's tipped to go far…
I've heard this place was the house of Karl Marx.

Marco recommends a ceviche of shark.
That, with the puree of artichoke hearts.
I dread to think! What's it like after dark?

What a hoot! They serve race horse tartare!
I'll stick to the stink horn and ripe Munster tart.
But this place was once the house of Karl Marx…

They say Michelin has dropped them a star.
Takeout for the Windsors – they send their own car.
I dread to think what it's like after dark –
did I say this place was the house of Karl Marx?

2008   MOSCOW, RUSSIA

MR PRESIDENT

I long to fondle the breasts of Vladimir Putin
as we ride back-to-chest over the Steppes,
my inadequate arms wrapped tight around him
stunned by the punch of his equine stench.

He eats curd of horse milk from under his saddle,
washed down with the blood he sucks from its neck.
When we canoe, it's him with the paddle;
when he dives through the plankton, I'll be his wreck.

Here in the Kremlin I'm spread on his bedstead
on the skin of a bear he trapped, skinned and tanned.
He wears silk and lace, skimpy and red,
my lips mouthing *Genghis*, his head in my hand.

2009   ROME, ITALY

A Letter from the Romans to St Paul

If you must have a god
let it be the god of wine

may the sign to your next brothel
be a cock of bronze like mine

and the powder on your nose
be of the marching kind –

may your pleasures be
the pleasures of the Romans.

When you go to the bath house
do not take a bath alone

spend silver on your mistress
but keep your gold at home

if the old dog is barking
then give the dog a bone –

may your pleasures be
the pleasures of the Romans.

Take a chance on Venus
worship mammon, praise the sun

why play for the wrong side
when our side's already won

we'd let you beat the lions
but the lions are such fun –

*may your pleasures be
the pleasures of the Romans.*

When you go to break your fast
share your dates among friends

don't keep your hands to yourself
if you've got a hand to lend

once the feasting has begun
may the feasting never end –

*may your pleasures be
the pleasures of the Romans.*

2010   ABBOTTABAD, PAKISTAN

Osama's Pyjamas

There was seldom cause to exit his pyjamas,
each hour was the one just before bed:
he'd gather the little ones to his chest,
whisper: 'Go west and follow your dreams...'
then distracted by the curve of a wing,
bird or drone, from below you never can tell
whether they've sized up your shadow
till that flash of heat seeking the ground
or a chop of the air in the darkling hour,
raptors hugging the nap of the earth,
air hot and high, Black Hawk down,
tap tap tap on your night cap and shirt.

2011 — SIRTE, LIBYA

THE PASSION

Had Mel Gibson shot *The Passion*
on mobile phones,
cast Herod as Christ,
armed the Romans with Kalashnikovs,
dressed angels up as drones,
and had the protagonist
dragged and beaten with shoes
from station to station
he couldn't have entertained us less.

They filmed this way of sorrows
as it happened, on location:
nailed him on the bonnet
of a pickup truck:
sodomy with knife was an innovation,
the wounds in each temple
made-up a face of several mouths
one of which opened
to question right from wrong.

Three days in that meat store of a tomb,
becoming the world's
most photographed corpse,
then disappeared
to wander the desert,
skin flapping from his bones,
hair a burning bush,
summoning the devil on his satellite phone
as if he's the last man on earth.

2012   BEIJING, CHINA

THE TEN DELICACIES

On a given day one year in ten
the Secretariat of the Central Committee
dye their hair the black of mourning
don their identical three-button suits
and gather in the Great Hall of the People
as those did who went before them
to mourn their elders' passing.

'For what you have done
and for what you have failed to do
we will never be sorry,'
they intone, beginning to carve.
The flesh has been fed well
and all the well-fed flesh
falls tender from the bone.

When their fine dining is done
the Secretariat of the Central Committee
put aside the banqueting tables
and drink their fill of yellow sake
performing traditional karaoke –
the party hymns they learnt at school –
naked as emperors the day they were born.

2013   TIMBUKTU, MALI

Blue Men Sing the Blues

The blue men of the desert
have no need of charts or plans

the borders on your map
are not lines in their sand

men that know no kingdom
are beyond a king's command

and the war for the Sahara
is a war that's yours to lose

if you take on the blue men
when they sing the blue men blues.

Like the last of the Atlas lions
they leave a trail of bones

and bones are ground to nothing
and nothing no one owns

when their drums beat up the night
you'll hear those camels moan

soon both notes in your head
will be written by an Oudh

then you'll know you've heard
the blue men sing the blue men blues.

The heartland of the blue men
is shaded like a bruise

where the blue men wear indigo
and indigo tattoos

but they don't mess with meaning
your ears won't be confused

you don't need to read a paper
to hear the blue men news

I've sung you what they sung me –
the blue men sing the blues.

2014   SEVASTOPOL, UKRAINE

A Disagreement Between Ukraine and Russia on the Nature of Poetry

A poem declares independence
and the anthology gets restless.

                                  A poem? What's left behind
                                  when the rioting has ended.

A poem's the first flag raised
just as the square falls silent.

                                      A poem is our army
                               on manoeuvres in mid-winter.

A poem builds its own prison,
a cell it can escape from.

                                 A poem has just forgotten
                                 what's given can be taken.

A poem as yet unwritten
is our new constitution.

                                   A poem's a loaded gun
                                 demanding your attention.

THE CARTOGRAPHY OF NIGHT

It begins in a house:
the house you are in.
Sit yourself down. Flip
open the screen. Wipe it
clean with a hygienic wipe.
Browse around. Like. Unlike.
Waste an hour shopping online.
Follow friends of your friends.
Rate where they've been.
Order pizza. It's pizza time!
Google the Earth. Zoom out.
Zoom in. Fix your sights
on a street now erased.
Rebuild buildings. Restore names.
Ignore a call from a charity line.
Click back time. Undo. Undo.
Send a selfie to your mum.
Flick the switch to satellite view.
Crack the sudoku in *The Sun*.
Tweet a haiku. Share it. Shout!
Turn the ticker, watch it spin
as the lights go gently out
and the dark comes rolling in.

NOTES

1914   Following his elimination of Franz Ferdinand, Gavrilo Princip twice failed to kill himself, first with poison, then with a gun.

1915   German officers sported duelling scars from their initiations in student fencing fraternities, some self-inflicted wounds.

1916   Of his abused and burned body, only Rasputin's penis was saved and preserved, a sure cure for impotence.

1917   If Tom of Finland had painted Lenin, it would have been on his return from exile at Finlandsky Station.

1918   The haemophilia of Europe's royal bloodline spread from the fertile womb of Queen Victoria.

1919   The influenza epidemic of 1918-9 killed 100 million people; 16 million died in World War I.

1920   The Cenotaph was originally crafted from wood and plaster as a staging post on the 1919 London Victory Parade.

1921   Churchill recruited war veterans to wage peace on Ireland; he is remembered there as fondly as Oliver Cromwell.

1922   A cut-up from letters to Henry Sinner, settler in Nebraska, written by his father Johannes in Norka, Russia, during famine.

1923   To send a postcard from Berlin to London at the end of 1923 cost 300 billion Marks.

1924   Duma deputy Vladimir Medinsky reports that communists worship only 10% of Lenin's embalmed body.

1925   At his speech to the Royal College of Veterinary Surgeons, Earl Haig proclaimed the continuing role of the horse in war.

1926   Following defeat in the Rif War, Abd el-Krim negotiated surrender to the French before leaving Fez for exile.

1927   If the Presidents carved into Mount Rushmore had bodies, they would stand 465ft tall.

1928   Like the House of Zogu, each royal dynasty begins with a man who crowns himself king.

1929   The Maginot Line is proof in concrete and wire that generals like to fight the last war, not the next one.

1930   Over 80,000 Indians were jailed by the British as a result of the Salt March, hundreds were shot in cold blood.

1931   Mustafa Kemal Atatürk, founding President of the Republic of Turkey, was named 'Father of the Nation' in perpetuity.

1932   King Abd al-Aziz, who married a daughter of every tribal chief in his realm, was survived by 22 wives and 45 legitimate sons.

1933   Wallis Simpson and David Windsor first made love on December 3rd 1933 in a roll top bath.

1934   Educated by Jesuits, Robert Mugabe has attended the inaugurations and funerals of successive popes.

1935   Under house arrest, Gorky was presented with a special edition of *Pravda* purged of all mention of purges.

1936   While Lorca died aged 38, his executioners survived to become loving grandfathers.

1937   Laurie Lee was one of many artists and writers to fight in the International Brigades; we are fortunate he survived.

1938   Sylvia Plath was born too late to take tea with Mussolini; Ezra Pound was his regular guest.

1939   At the outbreak of World War I, Hitler was pictured by chance, or subsequent design, celebrating near the Field Marshals' Hall; in the first days of World War II, he narrowly avoided assassination at the site of the Beer Hall Putsch.

1940   The surrender of France in World War II was signed in the same wagon-lit in which Germany had surrendered in World War I.

1941   The American economy grew by an average 17% a year during World War II, fuelled by a consumer boom.

1942   During the Exeter Blitz, the inhabitants of the city followed the rats to the marshes, forests and hills that surround it.

1943   The student leaders of The White Rose were executed for treason; this is a cut-up of their broadsides.

1944   Only whites among the Free French forces were permitted to liberate Paris; troops from African colonies were held back.

1945   Hitler had the cyanide intended to kill him tested on Blondi; her pups were shot in the trench where all were burned.

1946   The birthday poems of Emperor Hirohito were published on the front page of each national newspaper.

1947   While Lady Mountbatten entertained Nehru, her husband stuck to his serving boys.

1948   In 2013 Gandhi's portable spinning wheel was auctioned for over £100,000.

1949   Three wars were to follow the New Year's Day ceasefire including the first between nuclear powers India and Pakistan.

1950 A cut-up of kitchen advertising from the 1950s, an era when acts of consumption were considered anti-Communist.

1951 In 1951, the six inner states of the European Union signed the Treaty of Paris; peace has reigned ever since.

1952 33 when she died, it was another 19 years before Eva Perón was laid to rest, a journey in death remarkable as her life.

1953 As Tito said, Stalin is known the world over for his moustache, but not for his wisdom.

1954 In this adaptation of a Kikuyu parable, the panga is an East African machete; the British preferred bullets from a gun.

1955 Joseph Conrad's novella *Heart of Darkness* anticipated this poem by over a century.

1956 Only women were permitted to beat Winston Churchill at Six-Pack Bezique.

1957 Greatest of the Soviet space dogs, Laika was a stray mongrel snatched from the streets of Moscow.

1958 Van Cliburn is the only musician ever to have received a New York ticker tape parade.

1959 Sam's veterinarian described the reunion between the first space 'monkey and his mate' as "almost human."

1960 A cut-up of kitchen advertising from the early 1960s, an era when the domestic space was becoming political.

1961 On 17th October, up to 300 French Algerians were butchered by Parisian police under the command of Maurice Papon.

1962 The bearded Fidel Castro outlasted nine smooth-chinned American presidents.

1963 Conspiracy theorists neglect the coincidence of an international clown convention that day in Dallas.

1964 This poem is stolen from writers of the Hungryalist Movement of Bengal who were persecuted and jailed for their work.

1965 More than a million communists were murdered in Indonesia, one thousand at the hands of Anwar Congo.

1966 When His Imperial Majesty Emperor Haile Selassie visited Jamaica, he wore stacked shoes.

1967 The hands of Che were amputated for identification purposes, then repatriated by a Bolivian double agent.

1968 The events of May 1968 involved 11,000,000 striking workers, supporting student occupations for two continuous weeks.

1969 Ho Chi Minh promised: "If the Americans want to make peace, we shall invite them to afternoon tea."

1970 When the Jamaican Prime Minister stamped his foot at Lulu, the chihuahua roared like a lion.

1971 The Shah of Iran celebrated 2,500 years of Persian Empire with presidents and kings; he was deposed 6 years later in an Islamic Revolution led by the Ayatollah Khomeini.

1972 Pandas are loaned, not given; when a panda dies, its Chinese keepers return to collect the body.

1973 On receiving his Nobel Prize, Neruda declared "A poet is at the same time a force for solidarity and for solitude."

1974 The last of the Zanryu Nipponhei, Hiroo Onoda returned a hero to Japan, a country he no longer knew.

1975 During Christmas 1975, the President of Equatorial Guinea had 150 opponents executed by goons in Santa costumes.

1976 The coronation of Emperor Bokassa consumed one-third of his country's Gross National Product.

1977 That Christmas The Sex Pistols played 'God Save the Queen' before a crowd of cake-throwing children of striking firemen.

1978 The Bates family have not only ruled Sealand for almost fifty years, they also repelled a German invasion.

1979 The common man parables of Norman Wisdom as Norman Pitkin regularly featured on television in communist Albania.

1980 The Shining Path declared war by hanging dogs from lampposts in a pithy critique of Maoist revisionism.

1981 The 25-year retirement of Idi Amin was blessed with good health and the love of his extended family.

1982 President Assad studied ophthalmology at the Western Eye Hospital in London; he no longer practises his vocation.

1983 The BBC film 'Threads' depicted the effects of nuclear war on Sheffield, devastating a generation.

1984 *Under the spreading chestnut tree / I sold you and you sold me.* The song that torments Winston Smith in Orwell's *1984*.

1985 The Unabomber, former academic Ted Kaczynski, killed 3 and injured 23 in a bombing campaign of 17 years.

1986 The surviving 765 pairs of Imelda's footwear can still be viewed at the Marikina Shoe Museum.

1987 Following this exposure of weaknesses in Soviet air defences Mikhail Gorbachev was able to sack the military old guard.

1988 The first McDonald's in the communist world opened on 24th March 1988, serving Big Macs to the masses.

1989 When Nicolae Ceaușescu was exhumed, he was found to have been buried with a stake through his heart.

1990 To celebrate Nelson Mandela's 95th birthday, Indian barbers gave free haircuts to the destitute.

1991 Construction of the monument to Bulgarian communism was funded by compulsory public subscription.

1992 The hideaway of Abimael Guzmán of the Shining Path was exposed when police found packaging of his psoriasis cream.

1993 In solitary confinement before his execution, Saddam Hussein spent his days tending to a small garden.

1994 Kim Jong-il had a superstitious fear of triplets; like any dictator, he kept his friends close, his rivals closer.

1995 Of the two competing candidates for 11th Panchen Lama, the choice of the Dalai Lama has been disappeared.

1996 The Mexican capitalist press claim Subcomandante Marcos, Zapatista spokesperson, is Rafael Sebastián Guillén Vicente.

1997 Before he fled Paraguay, General Alfredo Stroessner considered building a retirement resort for former dictators.

1998 In the four years of Pol Pot's premiership, over a quarter of the population of Cambodia died.

1999 Visiting General Pinochet in his humble Wentworth home, Margaret thanked him for bringing democracy to Chile.

2000 The H'too twins who led God's Army of the Holy Mountain survived their childhood but now live on separate continents.

2001 Since 9/11, there have been 20 victims of terrorism on American soil; 365,000 have been shot by licensed firearms.

2002 King Zahir Shah's 29 years of exile followed a coup while he was receiving mud therapy for lumbago in Italy.

2003 The Iraqi Minister of Information became a figure of fun during the Gulf War; Alastair Campbell was taken seriously.

2004 The cause of Yasser Arafat's death remains uncertain though the symptoms were compatible with radiation poisoning.

2005 Turkmenbashi of Turkmenistan declared himself President for life in 2005; one year later, his heart exploded out of vanity.

2006 Following the failure of nation building in Iraq, Francis Fukuyama reconsidered: history might have a future after all.

2007 Karl Marx and family lived in 28 Dean Street, later site of Marco Pierre White and Damien Hirst's *Quo Vadis* eatery.

2008 President Putin welcomed homosexuals to the 2014 Winter Olympics so long as they 'leave the children alone.'

2009 Silvio Berlusconi was once a cruise-ship crooner; Julius Caesar began his career as the High Priest of Jupiter.

2010 In a 2010 video, Osama Bin Laden was filmed watching himself on television, waiting for the SEALs to call.

2011 When Colonel Gadaffi was captured cowering in a sewage pipe, he was gripping a golden gun.

2012 The 'ten delicacies' are mythical creatures deriving from profanities banned as keywords in Chinese search engines.

2013 Across the Sahara for as long as there have been states with borders the Tuareg nomads have fought against them.

2014 *Oh bury me, then rise ye up*
And break your heavy chains
And water with the tyrants' blood
The freedom that you've gained.
—Taras Shevchenko.

2015 The impact of war over time can now be measured by the diminishing radiance of electric light caught on sequential satellite images.

It is estimated over 200 million people
died as a result of human conflict
in the last 100 years of war.